Beddy Bye in the Bay
A Chesapeake Bay Bedtime Story

Priscilla Cummings · Illustrations by Marcy Dunn Ramsey

Schiffer Publishing Ltd®

4880 Lower Valley Road · Atglen, Pennsylvania 19310

Schiffer Books are available at special discounts for bulk purchases for sales promotions or premiums. Special editions, including personalized covers, corporate imprints, and excerpts can be created in large quantities for special needs. For more information contact the publisher:

Published by Schiffer Publishing Ltd.
4880 Lower Valley Road
Atglen, PA 19310
Phone: (610) 593-1777; Fax: (610) 593-2002
E-mail: Info@schifferbooks.com

For the largest selection of fine reference books on this and related subjects, please visit our web site at *www.schifferbooks.com*
We are always looking for people to write books on new and related subjects. If you have an idea for a book please contact us at the above address.

This book may be purchased from the publisher.
Include $5.00 for shipping.
Please try your bookstore first.
You may write for a free catalog.

In Europe, Schiffer books are distributed by
Bushwood Books
6 Marksbury Ave.
Kew Gardens
Surrey TW9 4JF England
Phone: 44 (0) 20 8392 8585; Fax: 44 (0) 20 8392 9876
E-mail: info@bushwoodbooks.co.uk
Website: www.bushwoodbooks.co.uk

ISBN: 978-0-7643-3450-4
Printed in China

Dedication

For Sophie, Avery, and Sullivan
and also for Camden and Rory

When it's time for good night, beddy bye in the Bay,
Every animal sleeps in a different way.

They may not wear pajamas or slippers like you,
But they love to be warm, safe, and comfortable, too.

In the Hookery Rookery Townhouse and tree,
Several herons built nests where they sleep peacefully.

There are nests way up high. There are nests further down.
It's an up and a down kind of blue heron town.

You would think that a nest tippy top would be frightful,
But the herons all say that the height is delightful.

When it's time for good night, beddy bye in the Bay,
There are some who choose mud as a good place to stay.

Crabs and clams love the mud. They will tell you it's grand.
They sleep best underwater in mud, grass, and sand.

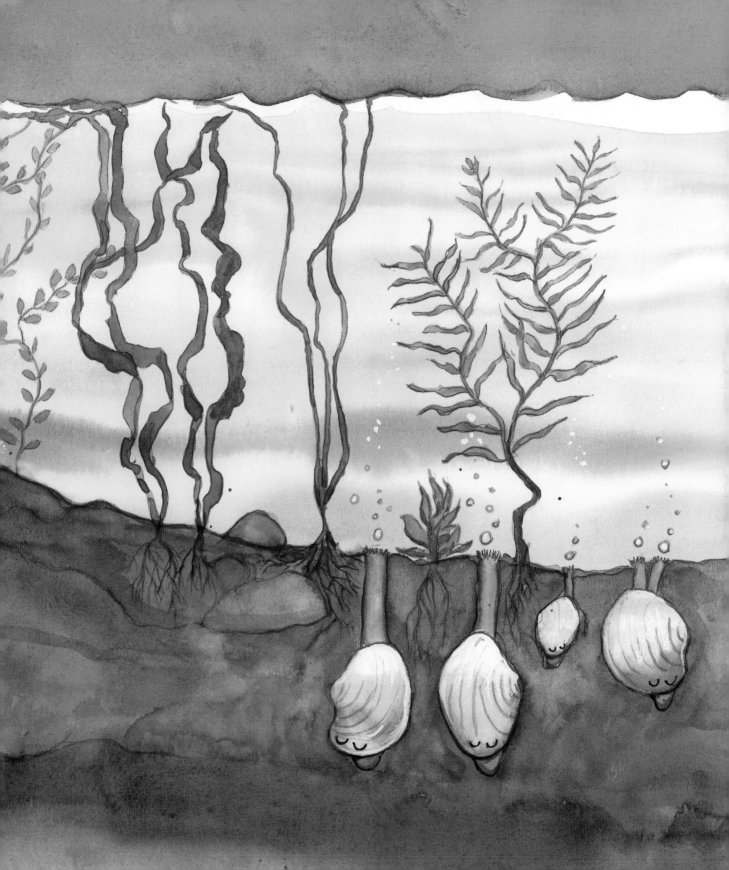

Mr. Turtle likes mud, but he also likes sun.
He takes naps on a rock in the river for fun.

How do fish rest their fins at the end of the day?
Underwater, fish slumber their own special way.

Since they haven't got eyelids, it seems fish don't sleep,
But the fish are still dreaming in hide-outs down deep.

Some fish sleep near a rock or beneath a big boat.
Others find a small cave, while still others just...float!

When it's time for good night, beddy bye in the Bay,
Ducks and geese take their naps in the one-legged way.

"Tuck it up! Rest your head on your back!" they all shout.
"This is truly the best way to sleep, there's no doubt!"

Just for fun you should try it. First, take off your shoes.
On one leg...turn your head...shut your eyes...and then snooze!

When it's time for good night, beddy bye in the Bay,
There are critters who hide without fuss or delay.

Pretty butterflies fold up their wings in the trees,
And then perch there so quietly nobody sees

In the morning the sun dries the dew from each wing.
They are drying and flying as birds wake and sing.

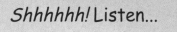

Shhhhhh! Listen...

From the Bay's creeks and rivers comes a *munch-crunch-kaBAM!*
The strange noise is from beavers constructing a dam.

All day long they munch trees and then drag away limbs.
They don't mind the hard work or the cold morning swims!

In their house made of sticks, tired beavers must sigh
As they curl up together and go beddy bye.

When it's time for good night, when it's time for a rest,
Lots of animals scoot to a hole or a nest.

But there's one little creature who lives in his bed
Without blankets or pillows to cushion his head.

It's an oyster — a whole bed of oysters — who prove
You can live your whole life and not once have to move!

When the sun finally sets, when night covers the streams,
When each creature is snug, safe, and ready for dreams,

Then it's time for a rest and an end to the day,
It is time for good night, beddy bye in the Bay.

The End

Autumn Journey. Priscilla Cummings. Cover Illustration by Doron Ben-Ami. Will Newcomb and his family move to Grampa's farm . A hunting trip makes him realize he is torn about killing a beautiful Canada goose. It is the tale of love keeping a struggling family together, in the face of hard times.

Size: 5 1/2" x 8 1/2" ■ 120 pp.
ISBN: 978-0-87033-606-5 ■ soft cover ■ $12.95

Beetle Boddiker. Priscilla Cummings. Illustrated by Marcy Dunn Ramsey. A tiny beetle that rarely leaves his house of leaves, one day needs to visit his brother, who lives in a rusty tin can across the street. Join Beetle Boddiker on an adventure that is not to be missed. Preschool to grade 2

Size: 9' x 9" ■ 23 color illustrations ■ 30 pp.
ISBN: 978-0-87033-602-7 ■ hard cover ■ $13.95

Toulouse: The Story of a Canada Goose. Priscilla Cummings. Illustrated by A. R. Cohen. One October day a young Canada goose became separated from his family on his first migration south. He and a lost snow goose became special friends for life. Their love story will be treasured by children and adults alike. Preschool to grade 2.

Size: 7' x 10" ■ 19 color illustrations ■ 30 pp.
ISBN: 978-0-87033-460-3 ■ hard cover ■ $9.99

Chesapeake 1-2-3. Priscilla Cummingsillustrated by David Aiken. Children learn to count with rhymes about life on the bay. "One girl went to fish, two ospreys fly high, ..." and the pages grow more crowded as readers approach "ten." Then see the numbers once again. The clever method and whimsical drawings will delight youngsters. Preschool and toddlers

Size: 9" x 9 " ■ 19 color illustrations ■ 30 pp.
ISBN: 978-0-87033-542-6 ■ hard cover ■ $11.95

Chesapeake ABC. Priscilla Cummings. Illustrated by David Aiken. "From "A is for anchor" to "Z is for a zephyr" the sights, sounds, and feel of the Bay come through to the youngest of readers. Whimsical drawings by David Aiken illustrate the verses about Chesapeake animals and things. Preschool to grade 2.

Size: ■ 9" x 9" ■ 43 color illustrations ■ 30 pp.
ISBN: 978-0-87033-525-9 ■ soft cover $11.99

Schiffer books may be ordered from your local bookstore, or they may be ordered directly from the publisher by writing to:
    Schiffer Publishing, Ltd.
    4880 Lower Valley Rd
    Atglen PA 19310
    (610) 593-1777; Fax (610) 593-2002
    E-mail: Info@schifferbooks.com

Please visit our web site catalog at *www.schifferbooks.com* or write for a free catalog. Please include $5.00 for shipping and handling for the first two books and $2.00 for each additional book. Full-price orders over $150 are shipped free in the U.S.

Santa Claws: The Christmas Crab. Priscilla Cummings. Illustrated by Marcy Dunn Ramsey. A feisty blue crab launches a rollicking Christmas Eve party that is interrupted by an unexpected traveler in need of help. Can the crab help bring Christmas to its habitat? Preschool to grade 2.
Size: 9" x 9" ■ 23 color illustrations ■ 30 pp.
ISBN: 978-0-87033-576-1 ■ hard cover ■ $10.50

Chesapeake Rainbow. Priscilla Cummings. Illustrated by David Aiken. Rhyming lines help young children learn their colors and facts about the Chesapeake Bay. A bright and wonderful companion to the popular books *Chesapeake ABC* and *Chesapeake 1-2-3*. Preschool to grade 2.
Size: 9" x 9" ■ 17 color illustrations ■ 30 pp.
ISBN: 978-0-87033-556-3 ■ hard cover ■ $11.99

Meet Chadwick and His Chesapeake Bay Friends. Priscilla Cummings. Illustrated by A. R. Cohen. The rhyming introduction to Chadwick, a blue crab, and his many bird and water-living friends, who share the bay beside the sea. Preschool to grade 2.
Size: 9" x 9" ■ 15 color illustrations ■ 30 pp.
ISBN: 978-0-87033-516-7 ■ hard cover ■ $11.95

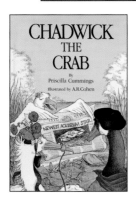 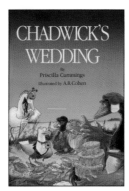    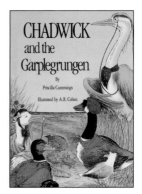

Chadwick the Crab. Priscilla Cummings. Illustrated by A.R. Cohen. A blue crab and its wide circle of aquatic friends yearn for adventure and the crab wants to be a star at the aquarium. This is the story of how one little crab realizes a very big dream. Preschool to grade 2.
Size: 7" x 10" ■ 16 color illustrations ■ 30 pp.
ISBN: 978-0-87033-347-7 ■ hard cover ■ $8.95

Chadwick's Wedding. Priscilla Cummings. Illustrated by A. R. Cohen. A blue crab is getting married in this rhyming story. But he has second thoughts and his bride disappears. The wedding is off and the search is on. Only then does he realize how much he loves his bride. Preschool to grade 2.
Size: 7" x 10" ■ 16 color illustrations ■ 30 pp.
ISBN: 978-0-87033-390-3 ■ hard cover ■ $8.95

Chadwick Forever. Priscilla Cummings. Illustrated by A.R. Cohen. A blue crab and a sea gull worry they will lose an endagered-species friend, a fox squirrel. Preschool to grade 2.
Size: 7' x 10" ■ 24 color illustrations ■ 30 pp.
ISBN: 978-0-87033-450-4 ■ hard cover ■ $8.99

Chadwick and the Garplegrungen. Priscilla Cummings. Illustrated by A.R. Cohen. What is the green and purple gunk bubbling up in their blue waters? A blue crab and its aquatic friends call the stuff "garplegrungen" (it rhymes with dungeon) and plan to get rid of it once and for all. Preschool to grade 2.
Size: 7" x 10" ■ 17 color illustrations ■ 30 pp.
ISBN: 978-0-87033-377-4 ■ hard cover ■ $8.95